PRAISE FOR OTHER WORKS BY A.W. SAM

- WASTE[LA]ND: POEMS FOR L.A.
- TOIL

"(A.W.) expertly weaves hope and despair ... winking and smiling through tears while he laughs. But you laugh and cry with him, because that's what life, and this collection, is all about."

- **JONAH RAY,** Mystery Science Theater 3000, The Meltdown Show with Jonah and Kumail

"When A.W. Sam invites you into his heart, mind and soul...GO."

- **JAMES URBANIAK,** American Splendor, The Venture Bros, Difficult People, Better Call Saul

"I love LA and I love the way A.W. Sam looks at it...Read this book!!!"

- **SARA BENINCASA,** Author of Real Artists Have Day Jobs

"A block by block LA odyssey of empathy by a multi-talented artist"

- **DC PIERSON,** Author of The Boy Who Couldn't Sleep and Never Had To, Derrick Comedy

THE PERPETUAL PLUMMET OF IMPERFECTION

THE PERPETUAL PLUMMET OF IMPERFECTION

BY A.W. SAM

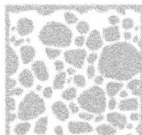

PUBLISHED BY:

GRAVEL YARD
BOOKS

THE PERPETUAL
PLUMMET OF IMPERFECTION

GRAVEL YARD
BOOKS

For permissions contact gravelyardbooks@gmail.com.

ISBN: 978-1-7378938-5-1 (Paperback)
ISBN: 978-1-7378938-6-8 (Digital)

Library of Congress Control Number: 2022914529

Printed in the United States of America by:
Amazon/Kindle Direct Publishing, Inc.

First Printing Edition: SEPTEMBER 1st, 2022

Fonts: Futura

1   2   3   4   5   6   7

Published by:
Gravel Yard Books
Los Angeles, CA

For additional information or questions please contact:
gravelyardbooks@gmail.com

"Have no fear of perfection...
you'll never reach it."

— Salvador Dali

TABLE OF CONTENTS

CONTENTS

FOREWORD

Hello and thank you for taking this journey with me. You know, my time on this earth, thus far, has been pretty interesting to say the least...chock full of joy, sadness, failures, triumphs, a few patches of good luck and a big stupid bundle of extremely bad decisions.

But if I'm being completely honest, and I am, (I mean, why wouldn't I?) I'm extremely grateful for every single one of my missteps because, for one, they allowed me to grow and be the person typing these words here today.

Failing and screwing up are as much a part of life as anything else but probably far more important.

Nobody's perfect, right? I mean, we hear that all the time, don't we?

Well ... here's the rub: what if the imperfect life IS actually the truly perfect one...full of endless opportunities to learn what life is really all about?

How boring would life be if we never experienced mistakes, disappointments, and shortcomings?

SPOILER ALERT: Extremely!

Our imperfections can make us feel like we are always falling but it's all just an illusion. Because with imperfection there is actually always somewhere else to go: Up, down, right, left, this way or that ... and even if it is down, eventually things have to go back up...or at least that's the hope. Besides, aren't bumpy rides way more exciting?

But maybe you already know all of this...

Maybe, you would just like to know that someone else feels the same way as you do. Well, I'm here and more than happy to help.

My wish is that the musings put forth in this book can help you find your own way through all the imperfect moments that lie before you on the road of life ahead.

Thanks again and I really hope you enjoy!

– A.W. SAM

THE PERPETUAL PLUMMET OF IMPERFECTION

THE PLUMMET

We're all caught in a constant freefall;
A perpetual plummet of imperfection.
For life is both a conundrum and a catch-all,
So, we must correct what needs correction.

Perfection is the poison we all desire to drink,
But why not quench your thirst with truth?
Divulge all those wicked thoughts you think,
And you may just find your proof.

The demons will dance inside your head,
And all the critics? May they be damned!
We cannot defy sweet failure's dread,
Despite our best laid plans.

Enjoy the ride, for now it's free,
Although soon, will come the cost.
But be sure to stop and pay the fee,
And relish all that you have lost.

Eventually though, the fall must stall
So, you can see the moment when...
To your surprise there was no rise
And the plummet starts again.

MORPH

I have died a dozen times
And if need be, I'll die again.
I've shed a coward's skin
And rose the occasion when

I needed to be reborn much better...
But there is no hero here.
I am just a loyal servant of change
And failure is the only thing I fear.

There are no headstones where
My fallen selves now lay...
No markers carved in stone to
Guide you down that wretched way.

Those bodies belong mired in the mud
And forgotten to time and space.
The only me that matters now
Is the one who bears this face.

BURDEN

Guilt is the heaviest thing I know
And yet it doesn't give me strength.
The more I try to carry on,
The more I keep others at arm's length.

One day that weight will break me,
Because the harm's already done.
And still, should I remain all tangled
In the spider's web I've spun?

Well, if the alternative is pain
To those that don't deserve it.
I'll bear the weight of guilt myself
And try my best to serve it.

THE LESSON

I'll never forget the first time
I saw a $100 dollar bill...

My father carefully
Took out his ragged
Weathered leather wallet,
Overstuffed with a thousand
Useless receipts
And not a single photo
Of his family.
He slowly removed
From the fold
A bill so crisp and new
I could hear it crinkle
As he held it out in his hand.
He presented it to me for inspection,
But as I tried to take it
From his steely grip,
He held on to it tight enough
That I had to really struggle to pull it away.
I would later learn this was meant
To show me that nothing good in this life
Was ever going to come easy.

AFRAID

I've been afraid for most my life...

Afraid to speak up when
I saw something wrong.
Afraid to do the right thing
I should have done all along.

Afraid to admit the harm I'd done
To those who deserved better.
Afraid to face myself again
Because my conscience won't unfetter.

Afraid I'm just not good enough
And don't deserve good things.
Afraid to finally find success
And whatever that may bring.

Afraid I'll get to fall in love
But then once again destroy it.
Afraid to trust another soul
So, I'll lie and then employ it.

Afraid there is no redemption
Once penance has been paid
Afraid I will never wake again
From this tattered bed I've made.

AFRAID (CONT.)

Afraid I'll be afraid forever and
Never allow myself to live.
Afraid I'll end up locked inside
Myself because I can't forgive.

Filled with pain and ample shame,
I think I'll sit and rest a spell...
Then drink a glass of cool reflection
Until all again is well.

THE PARTY

I sat down with my demons
And we talked about the past.
It helped me feel some mild relief
But I knew it wouldn't last.

They told me that they weren't quite finished
And there was still much more to do.
But I begged and pleaded for them to stop
And let me start anew.

They asked if I was sure
This was just what I really wanted.
But I knew deep in my heart
That I was tired of being haunted.

They vowed to leave but warned
They would return again someday.
Unless, I could show them I had
Truly learned to change my ways.

For now, they had to go and find
Some more poor souls to bleed.
So, I asked if I could think about it
And they said, 'take all the time you need.'

WHAT THE HEART WANTS

Love gives it all
And then tries to take.
Love brings down walls
But still shuns and forsakes.

Love can be terrifying,
Dark and treacherous.
Love can pervert,
Then be lewd and lecherous.

Love is a fuel
That ignites all the flames.
Love can be cruel
And taunt us with games.

Love doesn't care where
Or with who you have been.
Love still wants to know
Every one of your sins.

Love believes it always
Can conquer and win.
Love holds the knife
And then plunges it in.

WHAT THE HEART WANTS (CONT.)

Love bursts your heart
And explodes it in two.
Love is the best thing
To happen to you.

Love holds and protect you,
No matter the pain
Love pushes you down
As it cackles insane.

Love promises everything
And delivers you more.
Love can be selfish
And slam all the doors.

Love never really knows
What it actually wants.
Love hangs at all of
Your favorite haunts.

Love will support you
And help you achieve.
Love should be quite honest
But sometimes deceives.

WHAT THE HEART WANTS (CONT.)

Love is the pain
And the hurt we all crave.
Love carries the shovel
And digs its own grave.

Love wants what it never
Is able to give.
Thank God, we only need it
In order to live.

MEMORY

My memory is now about as sharp
As a limestone gargoyle
Left out laughing in the rain.

And while sifting through the
Quagmire of memories
I feel a shockwave fill my brain.

But is this lighting strike caused
By the last recollection I rejoiced in?
Or is the last bastion of my guilty
Conscience bombarded by inner voices?

Only the dewy aftermath may
Ever make sense of this...
Only the darkness may
Ever bring me bliss.

MAELSTROM

I've seen my face
On a thousand strangers
And often wondered if they know
We're all the same.

Am I so commonplace,
I can blend in like a
Discarded throw blanket
On some dusty bedroom floor?

I feel like a tiny thread
Standing at the ready
To unravel everything
If only someone would
Take hold and notice.

But what's so wrong with
Being ordinary anyways?
Doesn't it just make doing
Extraordinary things that much
More remarkable when
You finally figure them all out?

MAELSTROM (CONT.)

I'm worried my voice
May be drowned out
By a thousand angry shouts
Or I may fade back into the crowd
Like a drop of dirty water
Rejoining a pedantic puddle ...

...but it will only be momentary.

Because when I reemerge
It will be a storm
Unlike any you have never seen
And you will cower
As I wail like a banshee

and

     finally

          become

               the

                    thunder.

EVER FORWARD

Life can be kind and yet be cruel;
A winding and wicked illusion.
Thrusting us all into the void...
Down a road paved in confusion.

Where the road will lead us,
No one ever really knows.
So, try and choose the path less worn
And go where no one goes.

You may not like the things
That you will surely come to find.
But they are merely all the bones
From the selves you've left behind.

DIET

Pretending to be good
Is much harder
Than actually being good.

But on the other hand,
It does burn WAY more calories.
Besides...I do need to
Lose some weight.

I suppose I could
Just try to be good...
Ehhh, best not
To tempt the fates!

RUN

You could stand and wait;
Wasting your life away
For a worthless walk sign.

Or you can walk the line
And let it all go,
Running wild across the road
As fast as you can.

You just better have
Really good health insurance.

PARTS

A pair of legs can cause a car crash;
Even one they aren't inside.
A chain forged by some holding hands
Can make for change sometimes.

A hug can't fix the world but it can make
Your world feel right.
Feet can run a million miles
Or stay put and join the fight.

Parts are sometimes greater than
The whole to which they belong.
But exactly why, I just can't seem
To put my bony finger on.

VISITOR

We need death to call upon us
From time to time
To remind us life is brief.

To sit down across from us and
Let us stare down dark and deep
Into the endless blackness of its eyes,
In hopes of some relief.

Inside the reaper's soul lies a black hole
that may teach us how to really live.
For what lies ahead is nothing...
And that's an honest gift for one to give.

LED

Typing by the light of my laptop,
When I should have already gone full stop
And closed up shop for the evening.

But I'm stubborn.

When I close my eyes, I still see me
And all the reasons I can't sleep.

There's no rest for the restless but
The wicked seem to sleep just fine...
And one day soon perhaps I'll relax
When I finally serve my time.

At this late hour why does my mind
Start to race when it always finishes last?
Maybe I should take my mind to task
And ask it what it's really waiting for...

Ehh, it would probably just make another
Excuse and feed me some bullshit like
Everyone else. But in this land of the
Displaced and the disposable...

I'll take all the shit I can carry.

SHIELD

He often came home
When he was drunk,
Stinking of well drinks
And machine oil...
Possessed by some
Strange spirit that slowly
Made him forget himself and all
His sad little self-imagined hardships.

He never wanted
The three little burdens his
Bride had borne, but
He played his part in
Their creation so it
Also meant he had more
People in his life
To blame for his own failures.

In fact, the only thing
He made more of
Were excuses.
But you don't need to feed those,
And he'll make all of those he can.

SHIELD (CONT.)

There's no condom that can keep
Him from finding a fall guy
For his failures but if there
Was he'd probably pull it off
Because it wouldn't feel the same.

How did she get so lucky?

She has asked herself that same thing so
Many times, as she holds her lovely little
Ones close.

They are the light,
They are the lesson
And they are who she will hold the
Line for no matter what he lashes out with.

They are as much her shield
As she is theirs and
That is all she'll ever need.

SHADE

I do not like the light
Because I can be seen
Through twisted lenses.
So, I prefer instead
To stand just beside it
In silky silence.

Would I like to know
What it is like to feel praise?

Perhaps...

But I do not think
I will be so lucky.
So instead, I'll stay here
In the safety of the shadows.

Besides it's cooler here
And I can see everything so clearly...
Free from all the endless eyes that
Would eat me alive if they could.

But I won't let them,
Because I am not here.

REAL

There are as many faces
Found in wood grains
As there are among the stars.

They dance upon
The dew drops and
Glimmering hoods of cars.

But a visage
On clean countertops
Is no more real than, Scorpio.

For a reflection provides
Some keen perception to
Every single thing we know.

VOGUE

We all seem to wear
Shame like a shawl
When we could
Just as easily
Wrap it around
Our waists or
Fold it like
A pocket square.

It will still
Burn just as hot
As it sits
Next to our hearts.

Personally, I find shame
Quite out of fashion,
Especially when there
Are so many other
Better things to be worn.

But don't fret...
Regret never looks
Very good on anybody.

.

NIGHTHAWKS

I'll never be a nighthawk
But I know where they prey.
Perched about at some
Seedy public house
As the cigarette smoke

Surrounds
           them
                all
           like
                serpents.

Or over yonder sitting
In the driver's seat
Behind a silver steering wheel
Like they're on a stakeout.

But the only thing they're watching
Is the wild blur of taillights and
A life they can't quite remember
Buzz by.

Nearby there's an enclave
Of some kindred spirits
Singing in a diner booth banquette
While the staff stands by in wait
Staring down the clock.

NIGHTHAWKS (CONT.)

But these birds will
Either never notice
Or just don't care.

It's hard for much to matter
As the witching hours wane.
And maybe that's what helps
These winged wayfarers hanging
On to their wanderlust
Cloaked in the cover of night.

I'll never be a nighthawk
Because I'm something else...
Something broken,
That just can't sleep.

But I still know where they prey
And I really love to watch.

FURNITURE

I cascade down into the cracks
Of the couch cushions
Like a slick syrupy stream
And I see all your secrets here.

I could live like a king
Off this treasure trove
Of coins and candy,
But I won't.

Because for now...

Like you, I'm just a visitor
Exiting through the gift shop
Of this comfy and cozy filled curiosity.

Someday I'll return
To this firmly stuffed kingdom
And make it mine.
And you can rest assured,
I shall take my sweet time
Unearthing hidden hoards
Until all the stars in this sofa
Align once again.

ACCEPTANCE

I've often tried to lose myself
But I know where I hide.
Where deep regret and
Random guilt, both build up inside.

But lately I have welcomed them
And brought them in as guests.
There we put our bones upon the table
As we stare and beat our chests.

Guilt takes my hand and whispers
While regret firmly holds me down.
They then drag me to the waters
Where I begin to drown.

As water fills my lungs I wonder,
'Will this be the end of me?
Or will I find the strength to fight
And set the good I still have free?'

Then as it becomes the darkest
I gather all my might.
I rise and stare guilt in the face
And start to make things right.

ACCEPTANCE (CONT.)

I slowly gather strength
As air begins to fill my lungs,
And then I start to feel
The prodding sting of regret's tongue.

I vow to be a better man and
Live to learn from what I've done.
But before I can forgive myself,
I must start to walk, before I run.

SELF-LOVE

I don't hate anyone
More than I hate myself.
I'll forgive everyone but me
Because I never seem to see ...
I just sit there quietly and squirm.

Why would anyone care about me
When I choose to wallow in the weeds?
Why am I consumed with planting
All these hateful seeds?

I stare off into the dark and
I only see my face.
I cook for one and yet
Still seem to set an extra place.

I can't erase you or replace you
But instead, I state my case
In a solemn soliloquy.

Which still won't change
A single thing.

THE CRISIS

I'm much more a fool than a prince...
I take one look back at my life and wince.
I pile on more to my long list of vices,
Single-handedly put my own mid-life in crisis.

Half of my life is long, long, gone...
The reaper grows weary to play his song.
But he'll have to wait his turn to drag my soul,
I've fucked up just fine and heads must roll.

But not mine I fear, I hold on tight.
This isn't the first time I've had to fight.
It won't be the last though, I'm afraid...
I've still a hand left to be played.

I'll lay them out across the table
And stand up tall when I am able.
Though dark storm clouds still lie ahead...
I'll worry about them once I am dead.

BALANCING ACT

I lost my mind somewhere
In my last few relationships.
I found a little weight
In a few of them that followed.

I forgot who I was in you
But eventually remembered
In someone else. All it took was
A little learning to be selfless.

I quit living in the past
And started living in the
Moment immediately after I searched
Through all your pictures.

I still call out your name in dreams
Until I finally listen to myself
At last, and walk off
Into the next nothing.

THIRSTY

Without love we're truly nothing
Close to what we can really be.
But that love should not define us;
Only strengthen what are we.

It's only when I'm drowning
That I can finally breath.
It's only when I'm burning
That I feel truly free.

When I drink the water
Is when most I feel the thirst.
When I taste forbidden fruit
Is when I feel empty first.

So, for now I'll let love rule me
And see where it may go.
For I'd rather follow blindly,
Then never ever know.

THE DANCE

A stolen glance across the room
A shuffle of some feet...
Oh, how the wild wallflowers grow
And bring them both to meet.

An auburn bang is brushed aside,
A suspender snapped in place.
A mantra is repeated as
Her gaze locks upon his face.

The breath between them lessened
And yet a chasm still remained;
A surging sea of someone else's,
Caused this rendezvous to strain.

Palms growing ever clammy
As the night hour grows so late.
Would they ever come together,
And let sweet destiny seal its fate?

When the moment was met so suddenly,
He'd no words left to say.
Her tongue too was caught by cats
And yet ... there, both vowed to stay.

THE DANCE (CONT.)

The ether swirled around them
Like a vortex made of string.
And still their silence spoke in spirit
Though they never said a thing.

From a pouch, a rose revealed
All worn and wilted there...
Handed off, it danced its way
And bonded this young pair.

When the music finally faded
They turned and walked away.
Perhaps, wallflowers grow their best
Away from where they play.

SEAGLASS

Even the sharpest piece of glass
Eventually becomes smooth
If you toss it in the sea.

Spend your life in the sands
Of a rough surf long enough
And you'll grow so dull,
You simply cease to be.

WORST

I didn't find out who I was
Until I was at my worst.
I drank the wine from spoiled vines
And nearly died of thirst.

In the depths where I felt darkest
Is when I longed to see the light.
I'd never noticed it had gone,
Though I'd long possessed the sight.

Redemptions kiss lies just ahead
As long as you still try.
And knowing that should be enough
To help us all get by.

SOLAR

A palette of pastels
Spilled across the sky
And in the blinding light
Of your magenta glowing eye,
I found a quiet peace
That I've never known before.

A comfort that's been hiding patiently
Behind some old locked door.
It's hard to think such beauty
Was just some random rich creation
And not a gift made just for me
For my own appreciation.

How selfish is it for me to think
This ball of light
Was mine and mine alone.
I'd sleep better knowing
Its warm glow was
A thing to call my own.

For now, I'll share this amber ball,
So, enjoy it while you can.
Because one day it will only shine
Down upon just one man.

TWINKLE

I look up at the night sky and see
An infinite ocean of glittering
Eyes blinking back at me.

I wonder what they think,
I wonder how I look,
To these faceless interstellar
Eyes am I just an open book?

If they bore ill-will toward me
Perhaps I've never seen them show
Besides they're a million zillion miles away
And what the hell do they know?!

SIGHT

I have seen despair in tear drops
Cascading down dust-covered cheeks.
I have seen hope head for higher ground
When all feels lost and bleak.

I have felt the floorboards fade away
And slowly start to sink.
I've heard the hammer click
And placed the barrel where I think.

But I've also seen the sunrise break
The dark of morning dread.
I have seen some gone while some hold on
And raised my tired head.

There's only one sweet chance to make
Each heartbeat count against the sands
To do some good with what we could
And lift up these tired hands.

So, lift the cloak of discontent
And hold your brothers high.
For with the love of hearts like ours,
We can surely reach the sky.

READ

I often turn the page
But end up flipping back again.
So, what's the point of turning leaves
If you'll always remember when?

Some stories have sad endings and
I'm afraid mine will be one of them.
Could my own book be so cruel that it
Stabs me with the pen?

I will close the cover before I finish
To spare myself the truth.
But one day when I'm finally gone,
This parchment will bear no proof.

REPEAT

I have seen those eyes before
And they scare me.
The frame may have changed,
But they still have a malice that
Seeks me out like a missile.

They still drop all my defenses
Like an unsuspecting ambassador
About to be ambushed by an old friend.
Of course, I see it coming from a mile away
But I would let those eyes disarm me
Over and over again.

It's only a matter of time before
I am left lying on the ground.
But once I regain my composure
I will seek to find them on an all-new face
And let them make my life a living hell
Again ... and love every minute of it.

THE STRAY

The silent dread of a conversation
That you know you cannot win.
Not quite knowing why you did
The things that did you in.

Through tears you try and say the words
But they now fall upon deaf ears.
A single lapse of judgement can't
Erase all of those long years.

The moment that the deed was done
You fell on your knees and prayed.
Love forgives but can't forget the
Indiscretion that was made.

You swear you'll never stray again
As long as you shall live.
You vow to bow to any god
That has one more chance to give.

Gods aren't real but people are,
And they want vengeance to be paid.
Was it worth all the pain and shame you
Caused, the moment you betrayed?

THE STRAY (CONT.)

You'll ask that question many times
As you try to learn and grow.
But no matter how you work it out,
The answer's always: No.

MATINEE

Flooring coated in a
Sticky candy cum
That makes my shoes
Almost climb off my feet like
A prisoner escaping incarceration
With every solemn step.

A couple kisses behind me
As though they both forgot
All the reasons they shouldn't
Be together but it doesn't matter.

Nothing a seventy-foot screen
Can't sweep under the rug
For a few hours.

There's something magical
Happening at a matinee.
We all came here to hide
From ourselves and watch
Someone else make the mistakes
For once.

We'll all shuffle out at the end,
Back into the light of day once more
And head back to whatever hell
We were granted a reprieve from.

MATINEE (CONT.)

As we look up and check the clock,
We will notice a little
Popcorn butter on our
Pants leg and then smile.

That's never coming out...
And it never should.

LYRIC

A single song note can
Whisp me back to bed with you.
And a lyric lingering in my mind
Can hold me down with both
Arms as I cry my eyes out.

Music is much too powerful for
Us mere mortals and makes us
Pay for it with every single song.

In an instant, I'm in the back seat
Sandwiched between simple little siblings
While my parents play verbal ping-pong.

And then I'm there in a two-door hatchback
With my best friends screaming at the moon
As we cruise contently along without
Concern for how forgettable this will all
Seem until a song sparks it a new life.

These harmonious reminders haunt me
And I hope a new song can be used to
One day make a more favorable
Mirror into my soul.

WARRIOR

Justice is a long broad blade
That cuts both dull and sharp.
We seek it for the truth and those
Who stroke a vengeful harp.

But justice never seems to bring
The peace we hope it does.
It may just pluck and still procure
The pain that always was.

HEALING 101

Our pain is not unique
But we'd like it to be so.
Something no one understands
Or will never ever know.

But we share more pain than we do not
And should learn to talk it out.
Share your mind and you will find
That's what healing's all about.

THE DEAL

We're not prepared to deal with
All that life can throw our way.
But perhaps that is the point
So we can grow some more each day.

I don't know more about the world,
Than any other person.
And the more I try to change myself
The more things seem to worsen.

So, do I try then and just be myself?
And if so, who the hell is that?
Do I begin to go for strolls in parks
Or buy a brand new dog or cat?

I may not know who I am
Or what I'm supposed to do.
But there is one thing that I have found
That may just interest you.

Not making choices and holding back
Is not living much at all.
And the more you choose to do things
The more likely you will fall.

But enjoy the fall, or curse its name
It doesn't matter either way.
What does though is you made a choice
And lived to fall another day.

51

FOCUS

At my graduation ceremony
The commencement speaker said
We would always remember this day
But most likely not remember the shoes
We were wearing.

So, I made it my mission
To never forget those shoes.

Now it's been twenty years
And I can picture every part of those shoes
But not a single detail about
The rest of her speech...

...eh, probably unimportant.

GREENER

I've had nothing and been content
And I've had money but been miserable.
So why then does currency have the power
To make things so divisible?

Perhaps it's thinking what could be
Instead of living now,
Or forgetting that there's more to life
Or worrying 'bout 'the how.'

Because "the how" will happen or it won't
And that will be just fine.
I'd rather focus on what is
And better spend my time.

With that said I'd love have
A fancy dinner once or twice.
So, in fact, now that I really think ...
Some money would be nice.

PRONE

I've almost been killed in a crosswalk
But then laughed and walked away.
I guess I thought, 'It's not my time;
I'll live another day.'

I've dropped the ball and paid the price
When I could have had it all.
But then I would not have met you
As I got up from the fall.

Are we two reckless little peas
Stuck inside a little pod?
Meant to stumble here and there,
Oh no, here I go again ... OH GOD!

I'm fine, it's just a little scratch.
Oh, please don't worry about me.
Just plan to visit the ER,
And know how happy we will be.

PARALLEL

In another universe I was better
And the moon was always blue.
I never veered off from the path
Or did things I shouldn't do.

Night was day and day was night
And salty tasted sweet
I rose the ranks on my own merit;
Carried along by my own two feet.

'Goodbye' meant I'd see you soon
And 'Hello' meant never more.
I wish I could reach that place
And be the one that you adore.

Until then I will just pretend
That up is really down.
And know what it is I truly mean
When I wear this frown.

ROCK

I am a rock and so are you.

We are found in all colors,
Shapes and sizes
And are often extremely rough
Around the edges.
We are all at once
Perfect and imperfect
And always capable
Of breaking through
Just about any situation
We can be thrown
Into as long as we try.
And try we must.

I am a rock and so are you.

CREATE

I must create.

When the day drags on long, I create.
When I hear a familiar song, I create.
When the sun screams 'oh hello,' I create.
When the sun must finally go, I create.

I don't wait for that moment or
Hold out for the one,
I sit and when the feeling comes
I create until I'm done.

When everything is good, I create.
When I never thought I could, I create.
When I feel down and low, I create.
When I want to just let go, I create.

I am like a factory
And must produce to live.
I pull from every part of me and
Give all that I can give.

I must create.

LE CHAT

She knocks over a glass of red wine
And I punish her with some petting.
Then she decides to take a nap on an
Heirloom from grandma's wedding.

The whole time she stares back at me
Unaware of what she's done.
Who has time to worry when
There's more damage to be done?

She does what she wants
And takes all she can.
I am just a simple cog
In the moving wheels of her plan.

She's as soft as silk and a
Clawed, toothed velveteen glove.
But she's shown me that destruction
Can be a way of showing love.

THE HARBINGER

I sat down on a bench beside a man
And he began to speak
His labored voice and tempered pace
Informed me he was weak.

He said that he was ready
To go from this life to the next,
Then asked me, 'what have you done?'
Which left me quite perplexed.

I told him I didn't understand
And he said, 'Allow me to explain.'
He then leaned in close and whispered,
'I already know and no, I'm not insane.'

His familiar face was now more haunting
Than it was just a short time before.
Had we been sheltered inside a room
I'd have made my way to the door.

He said, 'calm down and listen.
You'll want to hear this through.
I know everything about you,
I know everything you'll do.'

THE HARBINGER (CONT.)

'I suppose you're me before I die,"
I said most defiantly.
He scoffed and said, 'No, I'm the you
That could, but shouldn't be.'

'I'm here to try and make your life
Turn out much better than did mine.'
I brushed some crumbs off my pant leg
And said, 'Why? My life is going fine.'

He cackled and then dropped his smile
As quickly as it had came.
'Perhaps I arrived a tad too late, but
I suppose it's all the same.'

'If you try and make up time
For all the bad you've done.
There may be some redemption left
From this wicked life you've spun.'

I stood and said, 'I've had enough,'
And that's when he grabbed my arm.
'I don't think you want to leave just yet.
You'd be doing both of us great harm.'

THE HARBINGER (CONT.)

I sat down again, reluctantly,
And he began to speak again.
'I've been down this road with you before
And we need to make amends.'

'I've done the things you haven't done'
He screamed into my ear.
But it's the things you have already done
That will do us in I fear.'

'I've made mistakes and tried to learn'
I defiantly countered back.
'So, why then do you repeat them?'
He returned with an attack.

'This all must be just some awful dream,
And neither one of us is here.'
He said, 'Well this is where you're very
Wrong, I've been here twice, my dear.'

He sighed and closed his tired eyes
As tears ran down his cheeks.
'I knew I'd regret coming here
With my body oh so weak.'

THE HARBINGER (CONT.)

'All I'll say is this, young me
And then bid you fair adieu.
You can't un-change the past,
Though try hard as you may do.

So, take the days that you have left
And do the best you can.
Or one day you will come to sit
In the place where I now am.'

And when I was all alone again
Left to ponder his advice,
The only thing I took from it was
That old man sure was nice.

GONE

When I'm dead will you pretend
You knew the real me?
Will you stand beside my casket
And perform a long sad eulogy?

'He had a big heart and a fragile soul,
The type you seldom find.'
Or something else to that effect
Like, 'He was oh-so kind.'

Well, I may have been those
Things and more, who's to really say?
Not you, I hate to break the news,
For I was lying all the way.

OVERCAST

If the sun gave up each morning
As much as I would like to do,
There would be no birds or fresh new starts
And leaves soaked with morning dew.

There would be less hope and long
Dark days that never seem to end.
There'd be grit and grime and creeping
Time and no light for glass to bend.

I wonder if the sun would watch and smile
As we all drifted in the dark;
Longing for those warming rays and
Summers in the park.

Would it give in when it realized,
How much we all depend?
Would it feel remorse and set back the
Course, the lives it did upend?

The good news is that the sun must shine,
As it too, must come to rest.
So, remember burn bright like the sun
And always aim to be your best.

STICKS AND STONES

The skeletons in my closet conspire
To kill me every chance they get.
I open the door and let them in,
But I pretend we've never met.

I could try to promise them
A new body made of skin.
But skeletons only want to ruin
What you've built; that's how they win.

All these bones bet they can break me
As they plan and plot their scheme.
But I must never forget that it was I,
Who made them all so mean.

COMANDEER

We look for deeper meaning in the things
That often are just what they are.
Like if only that light was green, not red,
I'd be sitting in a totaled car.

Instead of letting life get in the driver's seat
Perhaps it's time for you to take the wheel.
Because if you ever saw life's driving
Record, it would change the way you feel.

CLARITY

Get a few drinks in me
And I'll tell you how I really feel.
The rest of the time I'm hiding for real
Behind a crooked smile but all the while
I'm thinking about why the world
Is always burning.

I can't do anything to put the fire out, for
Now, except maybe scream. I dream that
One day things will be better but I'm still
Not sure what it will be better than.

I pick up my glass again and shake it so
The ice rattles around inside it like the
Dinner bell for a tea party I was never
Invited to as a child.

As I order another drink the bartender asks
Me how my day is going. I shoot him a
Shrug and he says he knows the feeling but
He thinks he has the perfect medicine I
Need.

We are agreed and I continue breaking
Down my barriers one more glass at a time
Until I am asked to leave.

CLARITY (CONT.)

Somehow, I am relieved.

So, I stumble out into the street and try to
Remember once again...

...what I was so mad about?

DISASTER

I scratch until there's a scab
And I pick until there's a scar.
A step and repeat, I often meet;
A great mystery I've come this far.

I'll poke at the bear and kick the nest
I'll rattle the cage and be your pest.
Feed me and I'll bite that hand clean off.
That seems to be what I do best.

I've caught more flies with vinegar
And found that sugar brought only pain.
It's the moments when I feel most alive
Are when I've circled around the drain.

I revel in the rubble, and
Stick my hand straight in the fire.
A moment's peace and freedom from
Despair is the prize that I desire.

If that be the only award I can win
I will gladly run that race...
That I might finally win and wear
A smile upon this face.

EL CAPITAN

Chaos is the captain
That guides this weary ship.
The tattered sails blown by the wails
Of battered souls taking this trip.

The charted course gets worse of course
With rougher seas ahead.
Imperfect waves provide perfect pain
And fuel desires to be dead.

But chaos won't allow it
Nor disembarking from these planks.
Our legs be chained and though we strain
To offer up our thanks.

Where the journey ends, all depends
On how we face the universe...
Tethered to the weathered masts
And captive to this verse.

I choose to lead the mutiny
And be the hands upon the helm.
Though chaos claims it can't be slain,
It can be overwhelmed.

EL CAPITAN (CONT.)

As waters calm, I sigh relieved
Now that I am 'in command.'
But it's all a lie, my end draws nigh
Chaos has already made land.

CURSED

I keep on feeling like I'm cursed
But I'm the one who cast the spell.
This dark rain cloud above my head
Engulfs me in this solemn hell.

To break the curse, I'll keep on going
Despite what happens next.
Throw all my caution to the wind
And break this self-inflicted hex.

Things may work out or they may not
But I will live to rue the day...
If I don't try hard to fight on again
And carve out a better way.

ROLL WITH IT

If you laugh off all your mistakes
You'll only encourage them.
They love a good chuckle and
Then, when you don't expect it...

BAM!

They hit you with another
Knuckle sandwich.

So don't laugh when you fall.
Give mistakes nothing to feed on
And eventually they'll need
To move on and find some
Other poor pathetic patsy
Who will laugh at all their
Stupid little jokes.

ROUND UP

We are all withering weeds
finding our way between the flowers.

But in truth...

I'd much rather be a weed.

A weed will do whatever
It takes; wriggling or wedging
Itself in until it takes root.

A weed pokes out its
Thorns to protect itself from those
Who don't appreciate it.

Weeds are survivors
And doom be damned,
They can bloom
If they really want to.

A weed can take anything
You throw at it and
You can be absolutely certain:

They always come back.

HERO

I'm not the hero type
And I think that's okay.
But isn't that the kind of thing
A hero's supposed to say?

A hero doesn't look for praise
Or like to talk about themselves.
They keep all their good deeds
Locked away and kept upon a shelf.

At least that's what I like to think
Because I've been more bad than good.
There were times I missed my chance
To do much better than I could.

But what if really screwing up is
Merely part of the hero's path?
Perhaps, I can still become a hero;
I could still workout the math.

If I am able to right this ship
And turn my life around.
Maybe that would be enough,
To find some solid ground.

HERO (CONT.)

Until that moment comes along
The least I can do is try.
Not every hero in this world
Needs to always reach the sky.

APOLOGY

I'm sorry that I let you down
And hurt you like I did.
I suppose I could just blame it all
On my trauma as a kid.

But now that I am an adult,
I must atone for what I've done.
The choices that I made were mine
And I must own up to every one.

I'm sorry I was not the person
That you were looking for.
I'm sorry that I dropped the ball
When you were asking me for more.

I wish I had been better
And could go back and set things right.
In hopes that I could once again
Fall fast asleep a night.

I'm sorry doesn't ever mean that you
Must say that you forgive.
I just hope it brings us both some peace
And I can learn to better live.

HITCHHIKERS

Don't toss away the apple
When you find a worm inside.
They need to eat like you or me
And they should not be denied.

A fly only wants a taste
But you know where it has been.
So, why not break off a little piece
And then you both can win?

And if you wouldn't help a fly,
Would you not help your fellow man?
Always think about the little things,
Then do the best you can.

EXAMINE

A doctor's office
Seems like
The wrong place
To be reminded
We're merely mortal in
This human race.

We should find out
All the things
That can do us in
At a much more
Pleasant location.

Here's my solution,
And it should happen soon.
Dairy Queens should all
Have a consultation room.

VENTURE

Embark upon an epic journey
Set off into the setting sun.
Play hard until you're on a gurney
Just make sure your having fun.

Write a winning novelette
Or pen some poetry that stinks.
Scribe a rather sub-par screenplay
And pay no attention to what they think.

Reach until you can touch the stars
And don't worry if they're sharp.
Flap your arms and try to fly!
Or make a trampoline from a tarp.

The more you do the less you'll feel
As though you were missing out.
And that's the most important thing
That life is all about*.

*Also: TRY TO BE NICE.

THE ABYSS

Death is very real when you
Sit and plan your own.
Working out the small details
While you are left alone.

Standing at the jagged edge,
Staring off into the dark.
Will this be the day on which
You choose to disembark?

Or will you stop and recollect
All the moments that you lived?
The people and the places
Flowing through you like a sieve.

Step back and sit awhile, my friend,
Before you decide to go.
And you may want to stay much more
Than you will want to go.

DECEPTION

The little lies you tell yourself
Become the larger lie you live.
The lies you tell to others build
Until something has to give.

The lies begin to grow each day
While you feed them like a child.
And once those lies begin to age
They slowly grow more wild.

In order to release the lies
The truth must come and set them free.
It's only then that you will
Know life as it's meant to be.

WALK ON

I came across a sidewalk full of cracks
And other little flaws.
Then I decided to walk along it
After a moment of great pause.

I knew not how this random journey
Was even supposed to end.
What dangers lie waiting around the corner
And at each random bend?

But off I went along the way
And watched my life pass by.
I turned grayer throughout the day,
And was certain I would die.

And yet I saw each little moment
And it brought me all to tears.
Because I saw – from start to end – how I'd
Finish my remaining years.

When I finally reached the finish,
I saw I'd returned back to the start.
And what I learned was: the end is fine, just
As long as you don't forget each part.

GOOD

I never said that I was good,
I only said I'd try.
And now with each new passing day,
I ask of myself, 'why?'

Is good a trait that we inherit?
Or is it learned instead?
I'd ask the man who made his mark
But he is far long dead.

I search for goodness everywhere
And learn all that I can.
But good must be a thing you see,
That is led with loving hands.

I want so bad to do what's right
And would 'do over' if I could.
But now there's only moving forward
And doing what I should.

GOD DAMNED

Sisyphus cheated death and then
Was made to always push a boulder.
Atlas fought against the gods,
And the earth was thrust upon his shoulder.

Prometheus stole some fire and then
An eagle ate his liver.
Tantalus fed his only son and was banned
From drinking by the river.

Lamia was turned into a freak
For sleeping with your man.
Cassandra was given future sight
But no one believed her plan.

Minthe bragged a lot and then
Was turned into a potted plant.
Arachne became a tiny spider
Forced to feed upon the ants.

The point here is, no matter what
You'll always make someone mad.
Just make sure it isn't Zeus or things
Will probably turn out bad.

HALF-DAY

I'm drowning.
I'm lost.
I'm frightened.
I'm sauced.
I'm tired.
I'm hazy.
I'm napping.
I'm lazy.
I'm spent.
I'm joking.
I'm overworked.
I'm choking.
I'm quitting.
I'm done.
I'm leaving.
I've won.

PARTICIPANT

First Place is great because
You did better than the rest.
Second Place is not so bad
Because you really tried your best.
Third Place is also fine if you
Ignore the other two.
Fourth Place just means that
It's probably not for you.
Fifth place isn't really something
You'd really like to come in.
But **Last Place** is never least,
Because you saw all the others win.

But my question is:
Is this the logic losers use
To make it through the day?

Well... I guess it doesn't matter
Because they got a ribbon anyway.

NEVER

I've never seen a dragon
But I've seen a dragonfly.
I've never seen a unicorn
But I've seen rhinoceri.

I've never seen a phoenix
But I've flown there a few times.
I never met a Roosevelt
But I've held a bunch of dimes.

I've never climbed a mountain
But I've drunken Mountain Dew.
I've never caught a swordfish
But I've held a sword or two.

Never is just a state of mind
So, change the way you think.
But if that doesn't change your life
Remember: you can always have a drink.

FUCK IT

You get one life, they often say
So, get out there and live it.
If someone wrongs you, let it go,
Then try best to forgive it.

If not, then seek the tree of truth
And find a fruit and pluck it.
Then while you eat and anger wains,
Say to yourself, 'eh, fuck it.'

LA FIN

SPECIAL THANKS

To little Lolo, my family and everyone else who has continued to support me and all my endeavors over the years. Though I may stumble, you have always been there to catch me.

You are my rocks and I'm always amazed you can still tolerate me*.

*or at least appear to do so.

PHOTO CREDITS

Cover art and book layout by A.W. Sam.

ABOUT THE AUTHOR

A.W. Sam was born and raised in Chicago but is lucky to now call Los Angeles his home.

He has lived many different lives as a molecular and marine biologist, television producer, actor, writer and comedian.

Under the name, **Tony Sam**, he has performed stand-up all over the world and has written for and appeared on numerous television programs.

His debut comedy album, **Scaredy Cat** was produced by Stand Up! Records and is available wherever fine music is sold.

He loves SCUBA and his two cats.

Please follow him on
TWITTER & INSTAGRAM:
@TOEKNEESAM

THE PERPETUAL PLUMMET OF IMPERFECTION

9 781737 893851